We will go for a walk in the city.
It will be a long walk, but not too long.

We stop here.
We see so many people.
And the people go so fast!

Then we walk on.
But we do not go so fast!

We stop here.
This is the Rose Building.
It's so tall!

We will go in here.
Then we will go up, up, up.

Here's the top of the Rose Building.
We see the city!

Up here, the city is so small.
Up here, we can see it all.

We went walking in the city.
It was a long walk, but not too long.